Morris Jastrow

A Fragment of the Babylonian

Morris Jastrow

A Fragment of the Babylonian

ISBN/EAN: 9783337247126

Printed in Europe, USA, Canada, Australia, Japan

Cover: Foto ©ninafisch / pixelio.de

More available books at **www.hansebooks.com**

PUBLICATIONS OF THE UNIVERSITY OF PENNSYLVANIA.

SERIES IN

Philology Literature and Archæology

Vol. I. No. 2.

A

FRAGMENT

OF

THE BABYLONIAN "DIBBARRA" EPIC.

BY

MORRIS JASTROW, JR., PH.D.,

PROFESSOR OF ARABIC IN THE UNIVERSITY OF PENNSYLVANIA.

N. D. C. HODGES,
Agent for United States, Canada and England
47 Lafayette Place, New York, N. Y.

MAX NIEMEYER,
Agent for the Continent of Europe
Halle, a. S., Germany.

PHILADELPHIA:
UNIVERSITY OF PENNSYLVANIA PRESS,
1891.

A FRAGMENT OF THE BABYLONIAN "DIBBARRA" EPIC.

I.

ASSYRIAN antiquities sometimes encounter a queer fate after reaching America, and are occasionally as effectively buried here as they were before being taken out of the mounds of Mesopotamia. Thus a sculptured and inscribed slab from the palace of King *Ašurnaṣirbal*, for over thirty years after its arrival in this country, lay stored away in the cellar of a city warehouse, where it appears to have been almost entirely forgotten until it celebrated a second "excavation" a short time ago, and then, by that strange incongruity which so frequently brings precious objects to the wrong places in this country, was deposited in the Pennsylvania Museum of Industrial Arts.[1] Again, in Henry Stevens' *Recollections of Mr. James Lenox*, there will be found a chapter devoted to a recital of the strange fortunes of a dozen *Ašurnaṣirbal* slabs like the one referred to, and which finally found a resting place, or more correctly speaking, a hiding place, in the basement of the New York Historical Society's building.[2] One would naturally look for them in the Metropolitan Museum.

The fragment of the brick-shaped tablet which is herewith published has also a history of its own. It was obtained about forty years ago by the American missionary F. H. Williams, the same to whom Yale, Andover[3] and other places are indebted for their *Ašurnaṣirbal* slabs. According to my informant, Mr. Talcott Williams, his father purchased it from an Arab, while riding through the mounds opposite Mosul, shortly after Mr. Layard had begun his remarkable excavations there. The shape

[1] Peters, *Sunday School Times*, May, 1886. "Nineveh in Philadelphia." Since sold to the University of Vermont.

[2] See Jastrow, *Proc. Amer. Oriental Assoc.*, May, 1889, p. 138.

[3] Merrill, Bibl. Sacra, 1875, pp. 320–325.

of the tablet, the color of the clay, and the character of the writing, in conjunction with the locality where it was obtained, show conclusively that it must have come from the chambers in the so-called Southwest Palace at Koujunjik, which contained the famous "brick" library of King *Ašurbanabal.* Whatever was recovered from this library—some 30,000 tablets and fragments—was sent to the British Museum, and particular interest, therefore, attaches to our little brick as being in all probability the only piece that has found its way to this country, of the collection to which, as is well known, we are indebted for almost all our knowledge of the literature proper of ancient Mesopotamia.[1] The value and character of the fragment, however, were not recognized, and, until it was kindly placed at my disposal by its present owner,[2] it served simply as an object of curiosity in a private "bric-a-brac" collection. The measurements of the fragment are three and one-half inches long, two inches wide, with one inch in thickness. The color of the clay is a dark red. It has a remarkably smooth surface. The writing, particularly on the obverse, is very clear and beautiful; on the reverse, the scribe, it seems, was pressed for space, and the characters accordingly appear crowded, making the identification in some instances rather difficult. For reasons that will become clear in the course of the article, it is impossible to estimate with accuracy the original dimensions of the tablet. When I received the fragment, the reverse was covered with an incrustation which completely obscured the writing. Finding, upon scratching with a penknife, that there were characters beneath the incrustation, I entrusted the brick to the care of Prof. Edgar F. Smith, of the University of Pennsylvania, who, in conjunction with his assist-

[1] See Layard, *Nineveh and Babylon* (second expedition), p. 347 of the Amer. Ed., 1853. Rassam, *Trans. Soc. Bibl. Arch.*, Vol. VII, p. 41. Layard's words with regard to the tablets found in these rooms, that in his opinion they would furnish materials "for the complete decipherment of the cuneiform characters, for an inquiry into the customs and sciences, and, we may perhaps even add, literature of its people," are noteworthy for their prophetic force. That is precisely what *Ašurbanabal's* library has done for us.

[2] The fragment is now the property of Mrs. J. Royce, and I have accordingly numbered it with the initial letters of her name.

ant, Mr. Lee K. Frankel, B.S., submitted the side to a careful chemical treatment.

It proved remarkably successful, and I deemed the experiment of sufficient interest and importance to request Mr. Frankel to give a detailed account of the process, which he very kindly consented to do.[1] A second experiment undertaken with this fragment was the reproduction of the two sides by the Levytype process (Philadelphia). Its superiority to the ordinary photograph will at once be recognized, and I think scholars will generally agree in pronouncing the reproduction in every way satisfactory. The characters can be almost as easily read as on the original, and in some instances stand out in even sharper relief. The only objection to this method of reproducing inscriptions on a large scale is the expense involved, but it is suggested that by taking a wax (or other) impression of the sides of a tablet or cylinder and preparing the plates from this impression, the necessity of making a separate plate for each side will be obviated and the expense correspondingly diminished. At all events, and in view more particularly of Delitzsch's recent remarks on the importance of facsimile reproductions of cuneiform inscriptions,[2] it will not be regarded as superfluous to have called attention to this admirable process. Apart from this, however, the fragment itself merits the distinction accorded to it, as I hope to show in the course of my article. I begin with a transliteration and translation, and after a commentary on the words and phrases shall proceed to discuss its contents, which a

[1] Published as an appendix to this article. I do not know to what extent chemical cleansing of the kind described by Mr. Frankel is resorted to in the European museums, but in the case of many cuneiform inscriptions, more particularly *Ašurbanabal* tablets that I saw in the British Museum, I am satisfied that much can still be done in this way to render the writing clearer; and the remark applies to tablets in the University of Pennsylvania collection, and I have no doubt to all other collections. The same process, involving the chemical decomposition of sediments attached to the clay, was applied to a second cuneiform inscription—a Babylonian royal cylinder, published by me in the *Zeitschrift fuer Assyriologie*, Vol. IV, pp. 301-323—with similar satisfactory results. Experiments were also made with other specimens, and I wish to express my sincere thanks to Prof. Smith and Mr. Frankel for their interest in this matter and for the trouble to which I put them. To my friend Prof. D. G. Lyon, of Harvard University, I am also indebted for some suggestions in regard to doubtful passages on the tablet.

[2] Delitzsch and Haupt, *Beitraege zur Assyriologie*, I, p 185.

glance suffices to reveal as mythological; and I shall finally endeavor to make clear its relation to other mythological specimens of Babylono-Assyrian literature. Incidental to the discussion, I shall touch upon a few general questions regarding the composition and development of some of the prominent Babylonian epics and myths, which, while forming digressions, will not, I trust, be found without value and, in so far as they bear indirectly upon my subject, may be looked upon as essential to an understanding of the position to be accorded to the fragment.

II.

TRANSLITERATION.

Obverse.

u
al In-mar-ma-ru e-ri-b[*a*]
u-ma-am ša-di-i u-še-ri-d [*a*]
e-ma kib-si
u-šaḫ-ra-bu
u-ma-am ṣeri la u
re-bit ali
it-ta u-lam-man ma-ḫa-[*za* (?)]
a-na šu-bat il [*ani limnute* (?)]
[*murim*] *reš limutti*
ekal u
u-d [*am-miḳ* (?)]
ri-gim
ḫi-i [*ti*]
ki-i
tir (?)

Reverse.

a-ge
li
lip-ti ni

ša šakkanaku bel
me-lam-me nam-ri-ir
^{il}*Ea ina absi* [*liḫiṭ* (?)]
^{il}*Šamšu* (*sic!*) *li-mur ma-ḫar* [*šu-nu*]
^{il}*Sin lip-pa-lis-ma ana tukulti-šu*[*nu*] [*lillik* (?)]
aš-šu šip-ri ša-a-šu ana Ea [*ina absi*]
lib-ba-a-ti im-ta-li
nis(?)*-su aš-šu ḫu-bu-uš pa*
să a-na šu-uḫ-mud tak-li-me ^{il}[*A-num* (?)]
ina la a-dan-ni-šu id-di [*nu*]
a-na sa-pan matati ḫul-lu-uḳ ni-še
^{il}*Ea šarru uš-tam-ma-a a-ma-*[*ta*]
adi ša it-bu rubû ^{il}*Marduk ša um-ma-ni-šu-nu-te*
ṣal-me-šu-nu ša ina niše ab-nu-u ana il
ša ilu la i-ir-ru i-di-ḫu-u
a-na um-ma-a-ni-šu-nu-te lib-ba rap-ša
iš-di-šu-nu
uz-ni iš-ruk-šu-nu-te-ma katâ-šu-nu [*umalli* (?)]
šu-kut-ta ša-a-ša u-ša-an-bi-ṭu-ma šum-su kat (?)
ḳu-ra-du ^{il}*Dibbarra mu-ša u ur-ra la na-*[*parkâ šu*]
u-zu-uz pa-nu [*šu-nu* (?)]
bitu să ana šu-un-bu-uṭ šu-kut-ti ana ma-li-kut
. . . . *i-ta-mu-u la ta-di-*[*ḫi*]
. . . . *šu* . . . . *na* (?)

TRANSLATION.

Obverse.

The city Inmarmaru he entered
the animals of the mountain he brought down
with treading down . . . .
they (?) destroyed
the animals of the field he did not . . . .
the suburb of the city [he attacked (?)]
the boundary-wall he damaged and the city [he destroyed]
to the dwelling of the [wicked gods (?)]

the sources of evil . . [he proceeded]
palace
he . favored (?)
assault
sin
as

Reverse.

crown
may
may he open
which the high priest, ruler
magnificent splendor
Ea in the deep, [may he behold]
Samas, may he see their presence
Sin, may he look and to their help [come]
when this message unto Ea in the watery deep [came]
he was filled with wrath
lament (?) in order to humiliate (?)
which for the presentation of gifts Anu
out of season . granted
for the destruction of lands and the annihilation of men
Ea the king uttered the word
until that prince Marduk came on with his [numerous (?)] hosts
The image which I built among men for god . . .
to whom no god approaches, they drew nigh
to their hosts a wide heart [he gave]
their loins [he strengthened (?)]
understanding he gave them and their hands he filled[1]
that construction they built splendidly and its name . . .
the warrior Dibbarra night and day without interruption stood fixed before them
the house which for the splendor of the construction, for the chiefs of . . .
. . . they spoke, do not thou approach

[1] I.e., sanctified them or gave them power.

III.

COMMENTARY.

Obverse.

2. About the city Inmarmaru, which appears for the first time here in cuneiform literature, I have been unable to ascertain anything at all. Only with reference to the name I venture to make a few suggestions. In the vocabulary II R 31, No. 3, 71, and its duplicate, V R 41, No. 1 obv. 35, *marmaru*, written precisely as here, is explained to mean *reštu*, "first" or "chief." The word is evidently a reduplication of *maru*, and equivalent in force to the compound *mar-reštu*. Again, the element *in* appears in the composition of such names as the goddess Innina,[1] (*i. e.*, In and Nina), the mountain Ingina, (II R 51, 8a), Inzabtum (Strassmaier, *Liverpool Inscriptions*, p. 28). Inbanâ (*ib.*) from In and banâ, and I am inclined to add to this list Inbâ (*ib.*). There are some facts which point to an ultimate indentification of *in* with "Sumero-Akkadian," *en* "lord," "master," as in *Enki*, *Enlil* and the like, and upon this supposition we would obtain a satisfactory explanation of the name, assuming it to be thus compounded. The etymology would then lead us to seek for Inmarmaru on "Semitic" soil, and since, as will be shown, the fragment reverts to a Babylonian prototype, we may settle provisionally upon Southern Mesopotamia as the scene of action.[2] Furthermore, from the description in the following lines, it appears that the city was of considerable size, surrounded by a wall, probably, and with a "suburb" attached to it, both of which are

[1] Mentioned by the side of *Ištar* in the cylinder of Marduktabikzirim published by me *Zeits. f. Assyr.* (IV, 301-24), and in an unpublished tablet quoted by Delitzsch., *Assyr. Woert.*, p. 408, lines 2 and 7, which, by the way, settles the question of her sex and also her close relation to *Ištar*. *Cf.* also In-nin with the epithet *etellat* (ASKT, 94, 61).

[2] At the same time, *marmaru* reminds us forcibly of *ma-uru*, shown by K 4378, col. V, 1, to be another name for *Šurippak*, the scene of the Babylonian deluge, particularly if we accept Halevy's opinion (Z A, III, p. 195), which identifies *mar* in mar-KI with *mauru*; only, if there is any connection between the two, instead of taking *mar* as Halevy does, as a contraction from *ma-ur*, it seems to me more likely that ma-ur, *i. e.*, "Ship-city," is a "rebus" or play upon *mar*, which would thus be the older form. While, of course, this resemblance with *marmaru* as a reduplication of *mar* or *maur* may be purely accidental, still, taken in connection with other indications, I regard it as wortby of notice.

important indications for the period when the story assumed its present shape.

Finally, the opinion may be hazarded that Inmarmaru will turn out to be another and possibly older name for a well-known Babylonian city, much as Ma-uru (see note above, and Jensen, *Kosmologie d. Babylonier*, pp. 495 and 515, and Delitzsch, *Paradies*, p. 223) is another name for *Šurippak;* and more the like. But until we meet with the name again, it is idle to enter upon further speculations.

3. From Sargon, Silver. Inscrip. (Lyon, p. 52) l. 25, where we read *umâm šadê u tiâmat*, it follows that *umâm* is applied to the animal world in general, with the exception of birds. Schrader's remark, therefore (KAT,[2] p. 17), that *umâm* is equivalent to the Hebrew *b^ehêmôth* does not appear to be exact, inasmuch as *b^ehêmâ* is never applied to water-inhabiting animals. Nor is *umâm* in Assyrian restricted in its usage as the Hebrew *b^ehêmâ* to animals of large proportions. The passage in the creation fragment, Nos. 345, 248, 147 (Del., AL[3], p. 94), which enumerates in succession *bûl ṣêri*, *umâm ṣêri*, and *nammašši ṣêri* points to *umâm* as holding a place intermediate between the great beasts and the small insects, and finally, I R28, 31[a] is to be noted, where *umâm* is contrasted with the winged creation.

5. *Ušaḫrabu* may be either a plural form of the Shafel imperfect or a singular with overlapping vowel *u* in place of the *a* that appears in *êriba* and *ušêrida* (Delitzsch *Gram.*, § 147), and it is difficult to make a choice between these possibilities; if it be the former, it might either have some reference to the *umâm ṣadî*, or the destructive agent, whose deeds are here recounted, may be represented as associating other powers with him. In l. 8, we have the singular *ulamman*, which militates against the latter supposition.

The restoration which suggests itself as a parallel to line 3, namely, *la ušêrida*, would be acceptable were it not that *ušêrida* is invariably used, even in its metaphorical extension, with *šadû*, or bringing down from some higher place. Still, it may well be that a verb with similar force may have stood here. At all events, it is tempting to suppose that some contrast between mountain and field animals is intended to be brought out.

7. The occurrence of the expression *rêbit âli* in this connection is rather interesting. As is well known, Esarhaddon and Sargon make mention of a *rêbit Ninâ* (see the passages, Del. *Par.*, p. 260 and Lyon, *Sargon* in glossary), and the latter in one place, also of the *rêbit Durîlu* (Cylinder, l. 17). If the city here referred to is, as would seem but natural, the Inmarmaru of l. 2, a third instance of a *rébitu* attached to a city would be furnished. It seems likely that the *rêbitu* was originally the open space up to a certain distance around the city after the fashion of the "Haram" around Mecca and the mark or common in the Aryan village community, and only as the city grew became its suburb proper.

8. *Ittu*, in the sense of boundary, with the plural *itâti*, is applied to river shore as well as to the limits of towns, as the expression *i- it nari* (II R 56, 26) shows. The attack upon the city Inmarmaru is evidently described in these lines. The *rêbitu* is first assailed, then the *ittu* is injured, by which we are perhaps to understand that a breach in the wall has been made, and finally the city itself is reached. The *rêbitu* would accordingly be situated beyond the walls or boundary proper of the city. If the restoration *maḫâzu* be accepted—and there seems scarcely room for doubt—a further support would be given to Pater Scheil's (*Samsiramman* IV, p. 36) objections to Schrader's view (*Keils. Bibl.*, I, p. vii), that *âlu* is restricted in its usage to poetry, whereas the common word for city is *maḫâzu*—a relation, by the way, precisely the reverse of the Hebrew *ʿîr* and *mâḫôz*. The fact seems to be that while at one time such a difference as Schrader claims may have actually existed in the use of the two terms, later on either word was used indifferently in poetry or prose, just as the *formal* difference between a *maḫâzu* and an *âlu*, which it is but natural to assume also prevailed, gave way to a complete identification, precisely as we in English use town and city interchangeably; and so also in post-Biblical Hebrew *mâḫôz* is as frequent as *ʿîr*. To *êma kibsi*,

it may be noted that IVR 15, Rev. 6, the seven evil spirits are described *idât absî ana kabâsi idḫûni* "drawing nigh for destroying (lit., treading down) the shores of the deep."

10. My reading of the signs at the beginning of this line is suggested by IVR 5, col. I, 10, and col. II, 27. In both passages *murîm rêš limutti* is an epithet applied to the seven evil spirits, and since the expression does not occur elsewhere in a connected text,[1] so far as I am aware, it is legitimate to conclude that here, too, there is the same, or a similar, reference. One is tempted, then, to complete the ninth line as follows: *ana šubat ilâni limnûte.* The traces to be seen after the sign for god might very well be the plural sign, but what follows is entirely too vague to warrant an opinion one way or the other. IV R. 5, col. I, 51, there is a reference to this "*šubtu*" of the evil spirits, and it also appears from this passage that the seat in question over which Anu, the king of the seven spirits, presides is none other than the *šamû rapaštu*—the broad expanse of heaven.

So in the Hymn (K. 8235 and 8234) published by Brünnow (ZA. IV, p. 228), Anu is described as *âšibu šamâmi*—"inhabiting the heavens." As for the expression, *murîm rêš limutti*, it is clear that a literal rendering will help us but little. Lenormant (*Et Aec.* III, p. 122 and 126) proposes "complotant (dans) les têtes mechantes," which has the double defect of being obscure and unsatisfactory. Sayce (*Hibbert Lectures*, p. 463), "enlarging their evil heads," marks no improvement, while Hommel (*Sem. Voelk* I, p. 307) evades the difficulty by leaving the words untranslated. I take *rêš* here in the figurative sense which the word has in all Semitic languages of "source" or "essence," and render the phrase, the stirrers up,[2]—*murîm* being either singular or plural (construct)—of the very source of evil, or more simply, the "primeval causes of evil"—an epithet which accords well not only with the character of these spirits, but

[1] II R. 32, 24^{e}, the expression occurs in a vocabulary.

[2] The ideogram corresponding to *murim*, viz: ḪA ZA (evidently Semitic '*ḫz*), has the general force of *holding*, as *Del. Woert*, p. 301, shows. The verb *râmu* may, therefore, also have this meaning, and there is no reason for reading *mukir* in such passages as I, R. 29, 3, Asurn, I, 2, etc., as Scheil, (*Samsiramman* IV, p. 2). would have us do. See Jensen, *Kosmologie der Babylonier*, p. 245.

also with the phrase immediately preceding in IV R 5, col. I, 8, "*êpêš marušti šunu*," which would then stand in a sort of parallelism to our phrase, though there is also implied a certain progress in the thought. A free rendering would be "Evil-doers are they; nay, the very source of evil."

In accordance with what has above been pointed out, the *šubtu* referred to, if my restoration be accepted, would be the same broad expanse of heaven as mentioned in the quoted passages of IV R 5. The few remaining words of this side of the fragment are entirely too vague to furnish a clue for tracing the further progress of the events, but so much is certain that after the capture of Inmarmaru the scene is transferred to another place.

Reverse.

Ll. 1–3. The reverse of the fragment opens with an invocation to the gods. It is evident that, in addition to *Ea*, *Šamas* and *Sin*, some other deities were invoked in the prayer. The syllable *li*, in line 2, is certainly the precative particle attached to some verb expressive of a request of some kind, and on the supposition that *lipti*, of l. 3, belongs to a different subject, there would be five deities, at least, who are appealed to. In view of this, it will not be considered too bold to regard *age*, of line 1, as part of some such phrase as *bêl age* or *šar age*, and the title of some god. Now, while in the historical and religious texts *Sin*[1] (or Nannar) is the only one of the gods to whom such titles are applied, *bêl age* (IVR 9, 14. Tigl. Pil., I, 5, VR 1, 3) and *šar age* (Salm. Obel. 6), the crown, as such, is an emblem of divinity in general. So *Ištar* (IV R 68, 36, c), *Šamas*[2] (M. 192, according to Sayce, *Hibbert Lec-*

[1] *Ašur* has also the title *nadin ḫatti* or *age* (Tigl. Pil., I, 2), but the story being Babylonian (as will be shown), *Ašur* is, of course, out of the question.

[2] The *agu* (?) *Šamas* of the Aboo-Habba tablet or *kudur Samas* (see my paper on *kudûru*, PAOS, October, 1889) can no longer be admitted as evidence that the Sun-god has a crown, as Sayce (*Hibbert Lectures*, p. 285) takes it, for the word refers to the ring which the deity holds in his hand, as W. H. Ward has conclusively shown (PAOS, May, 1887). Both Scheil and Jeremias, in their recent translations of the inscription, ought to have taken notice of Dr. Ward's important paper. Delitzsch *Woert.*, p. 85, will also have to be corrected accordingly.

tures, p. 286), and *Marduk* (VR 33, col. II, 52) have crowns, and so also Bel is spoken of as *âpir agâsŭ*, "decked with his crown," while in K. 646, 7 (published by Delitzsch, *Woerterbuch*, p. 141 [1]) there is a reference to the "crown of Anu." The title might therefore apply to any of these, and, for that matter, even these would not exhaust the possibilities. It cannot refer to Sin, for he is mentioned just below, and again Marduk may be excluded from consideration, for he appears in a different rôle further on in the tablet. Now Anu or Bel (or even both) would fittingly enter as deities to be addressed in the appeal for help (*ana tukultišunu*, l. 7) that is being made, but this supposition, as will appear further on, would carry with it such important conclusions as to the position of the fragment in Babylonian mythology that it ought not to be admitted without satisfactory evidence. As for *Ištar*, a word must be said. In the tale of the seven spirits in the incantation texts, *Sin*, *Šamas* and *Ištar* are introduced side by side (see IV R I, col. II, 30–34, and IV R 5, col. I, 60), and so also on the devices accompanying the Aboo-Habba tablet (V R 60) *Sin*, *Šamas* and *Ištar* (with *absu* as representing Ea) are brought together. Further on, the connection between the story of our fragment and these episodes—extracted evidently from some collection—will be dwelt upon, and from what will there be said it will appear more than plausible that *Ištar* was among the gods here invoked. In her capacity as daughter of the Moon-god—so, *e.g.*, in the tale of the "Descent to Hades"—the title of *bêlit agi*, or *šarrat agi*, would be appropriate.

4–5. The translation of the words to be seen in these lines is simple enough, but their relation to what precedes and follows is not altogether clear. *Mêlammu namrir* might be the epithet of some deity and synonymous in force with *šakû namriri*, applied to Sin (Tigl. Pil., I, 5, and Salm. Obel. 6). *Šakkânâku*, the well-known priestly title,[2] does not appear applicable to a deity, but it is to be noted that in a tablet dealing with the

[1] See also Strassmaier, *Verzeichniss*, etc., p. 23.
[2] *Cf.* Lyon *Sargon*, p. 79.

ravages of the plague-god (M. 55, Sayce, *Hibbert Lectures*, pp. 311–312), it seems that the epithet *is* applied to that god, and, furthermore, IV R. 1, col. II, 45, the fire-god Gibil is designated as *ša-ka-nak.*[1] The latter deity may, indeed, be meant here, and the further designation as *mêlammu namrir* would accord well with the character of this god, who, for instance, is elsewhere described as *litpušu mêlammi*, "clothed in glory" (IV R 26, No. 3, 38). It is to be noted, also, that in the magical text ASKT., p. 96, Gibil is invoked against the evil spirits immediately after Marduk, while in IV R I, he is brought into close connection with the seven spirits as one of their opponents, and finally, K. 2585, (Sayce, *Hibbert Lectures*, p. 570) he is shown to be the direct enemy of the plague-god—all of which points to the appropriateness of his being introduced into our fragment. Assuming the above considerations to have a sufficient foundation, we would have, in the first lines of the reverse, a prayer for help addressed to the fire and water, sun and moon, with *Ištar* as a fifth, representing, perhaps, the planets or stars.

7. The reading *Šam-šu* for the sun-god, with the phonetic complement, is noteworthy, and our passage furnishes a welcome confirmation for the reading *ukallimu šam-šu* in the Bellino Cyl. of Sennacherib, l. 47, already proposed by George Smith, but rejected by Evetts (ZA, iii, p. 325 and Note, p. 330). Evetts' translation misses the point entirely. The words must be rendered "exposed to the sun," and the passage is to be interpreted in accordance with the suggestions of Jeremias' *Vorstell vom Leben n. d. Tode*, p. 52. Asurn I, 10 and Salm. Ob. 16, the phonetic writing, *Šam-šu*, for the deity occurs, though in both cases the other sign for *šu* (Delitzsch, *Schrifttafel*, No. 199) is the one used, but in the hymn ZA. V., p. 77, 34, the word appears written just as in our fragment.

8. The verbs *amâru* and *palâsu* are here synonymously used as frequently (see Zimmern *Busspsalmen*, pp. 17–18. Jeremias' *Vorstell v. Leben nach dem Tode*, p. 55). At the end of the

[1] Note, too, that the ideographic equivalent for *šakkânâku* enters into the composition of Nergal (Jensen, *Kosmologie*, p. 477).

sixth line we must also supply some verb with a similar meaning, possibly *lihit* from *hâtu*, which V R 64, 37[a] and VR 34. col. III, ll. 12 and 15, is found as a synonym of *palâsu*.

9-10. Of the gods appealed to, Ea alone appears to respond. IV R 5, col, II, 53-55, where Ea is informed by Nusku, the messenger of Bel, of the ravages and audacity of the evil spirits, the following phrase is used, which offers an interesting parallel to our passage: *Ea ina absi amât šu[atu išmê ma] šipatsu iššuk.* "Ea of the deep heard of that affair and bit his lip."[1] Again, in the same tale, Col. I, 54 ffg, Bel's feelings are thus described: *Inušu Bel têma šuatu išmêma amâta ana libbišu išdud.* "At the time that Bel heard the report, he took it to heart." Thirdly, in the story of the Deluge, when Bel sees the ship with *Ṣitnapištim,* as Jensen (*Kosmologie*, p. 384), would have us read the name of the hero who has survived the flood, there occurs the same phrase as l. 10 of our brick, *libbâti imtalî*, written precisely with the same signs, barring the omission of *a* after *ba* of *libbâti*. The recurrence of the phrase here disposes finally of Haupt's supposition of a possible clerical error in the Deluge passage (see KAT², p. 78).[2] The phrase is a very forcible idiomatic expression (literally "filled with hearts") for anger. A similar expression is found K 1139, 21, *mimma libbâtia la imallû.* In contrast to these passages, where the wrath of Ea is described, we have finally one where his joy is spoken of. In the creation, fragment 18, celebrating the praises of Marduk for his conquest of *Kirbiš-Tiâmat*, the "dragon," Ea, upon hearing of the glorious epithets bestowed upon his son, we are told, "*išmêma Ea kabittašu itêngu*"—"Ea heard, and his spirit (lit., liver) rejoiced," and he crowns the honors heaped upon Marduk by declaring that the latter's name should be Ea, just as his own. The bearings of these passages upon the story of our fragment will be taken up further on.

From a comparison of the above passages, it follows (*a*) that *aššu* and *inušu* may be used quite synonymously; and (*b*)

[1] In the "Descent of Istar," Rev. 21, *Ištar* bites her finger as a sign of her wrath.

[2] From Haupt, Delitzsch *Beitraege zur Assyriologie*, I, p. 131, it appears that Haupt has himself abandoned this supposition. He refers also to the phrase *ina malê libbâti*, v R. 7, 26.

that *ṭêmu* and *šipru* are synonyms.[1] There appear to be at least three different *aššu* in Assyrian, as follows: (1) expressive of a reason, with the force of *because, as regards to;* (2) expressive of a purpose, *in order to;* and (3) expressive of time, *when, at the time when.* In line 10, there is an instance of the latter, whereas in line 11, the second is probably intended. These three *aššu* must be sharply distinguished from one another, and although identical in form, they arise from a contraction of *different* elements. The first corresponds to Arabic *inna,* with the addition of the demonstrative particle *šu;* the second is the Arabic *anna,* with the same emphatic addition; while the third, I take to be a combination of the common Assyrian temporal particle *in* (*u*), with *šu,* and for which the uncontracted forms *inušu* and *inušuma* are also found.

One is inclined to believe that the attempt was made at one time by the Assyrian scribes to distinguish, at least in writing, between these several *aššu* by availing themselves of the existence of the two signs for *šu* (Nos. 199 and 294 of Delitzsch's Schrifttafel), and certainly I have come across no instance of *aššu* in the temporal sense written otherwise than with the sign No. 199, but between the other two *aššu* there now reigns a hopeless confusion in the texts, for although the second one appears always to be written with the *šu* No. 294, the first appears quite indifferently with the one or the other, and it is only from the context that we can conclude which of the two is meant.

Lines 11, 12 are exceedingly difficult. They apparently furnish a further explanation for the anger of Ea. None of the readings that suggest themselves for the first two signs appear satisfactory, and I suspect them to constitute some ideograph. While not absolutely certain of the reading *ḫu-bu-uš*—the characters are very much crowded and faint—still I feel quite sure of its being right. The stem *ḫabâšu* has not been met with frequently as yet in the texts. We have it in *ḫi-bi-iš-ti,* a word that occurs several times in the inscriptions of Sargon (see Lyon

[1] *Amâtu* also appears as a synonym of these words Hommel, *Semiten*, p. 308).

and Winckler for the passages), and also in those of Sennacherib (Pognon *Bavian*, pp. 64–5), though it is to be remembered that the reading *hišimtu* adopted by Brünnow (*List of Cuneiform Ideographs*, No. 5794) is also possible, even if quite improbable. For the Sargon passages, a meaning like "product" seems to be demanded by the context in all but one. In the Bull Inscription, line 41, and, also, in the Sennacherib passages, some species of trees or plants are clearly described by the word. Again, in the syllabary III R, 70, 158, we find *ḫa-ab-šu* in a group explanatory of No. 71 of the Schrifttafel. It is accompanied by a synonym, *ṣa* . . . . which, since the sign is explained elsewhere by *ṣararu* or *ṣaraḫu* (see Brünnow's *List*, Nos. 2986–7) is to be filled out accordingly, though *za*[*maru*], suggested by Brünnow (No. 2995) is also possible. But, after all, *zamaru*, sing, and *ṣaraḫu*, cry, are closely related in sense, and on the other hand *ṣararu*, oppose (?), and *ṣaraḫu* contain the same root, *ṣr*, expressive of some violent action. So much then may be concluded from the connection in which *ḫa-ab-šu* occurs, that it may have some such force as destruction or humiliation. Thirdly, *ḫi-ib-šu* is the specification or description of some garment in the clothing list, VR 14, 40^b, but, unfortunately, the left-hand column of the list is here wanting, and the words within which it is grouped are not of a kind to warrant any safe conclusions (*miṣru*, cut (?), *ḫilṣu*, strong, *šinṭu*, torn), though they show at least an accord with the general meaning, that we have hit upon for the stem.[1]

12. The meaning "present" or "offering" for *taklîmu* is sufficiently established by VR 11, 2^b, where it is placed between *nindâbu* and *kištu* (*Cf.* Haupt *Hebraica*, III, p. 109). Latrille's explanation (ZA, I, p. 37) from the stem *kalâmu*, to show, is satisfactory, and this further suggests a comparison with the Hebrew *pânîm*, in the phrase *leḥem hap-pânîm*, "shew-bread." The word occurs again, and is written just as here, in the mythological fragment K, 2087, 8 (published by Sayce, Trans. Soc. Bibl. Arch., IV, pp. 305–6) where it appears to be used in paral-

[1] Assuming a Semitic origin, which seems more than likely, we have the stem also in the mountain, *Ḫubšân*, mentioned IIR 60, 7b. Does the same element perhaps lurk in *Ḫubuškia*?

lelism with *dumku*, which furnishes a further confirmation of its meaning. And so also in the hymn to Marduk, published by Brünnow (ZA, IV, pp. 36-9), we have the singular form *tanâmdin taklîma ana dariš*, "thou grantest a present eternally." A different word, though closely related, is *taklîmtu*, shown by VR 22^{b}, to be a synonym of *têrtu*, law, and which, therefore, upon the supposition of a derivation from "show" is the exact parallel of our word "revelation." There is no doubt that we have the plural of this word in *tak-la-ma-at* on one of the Tel-el-Amarna tablets (PSBA, xi, p. 332) though Sayce reads *tag-la-ma-at*, and moreover confesses the word with *taklîme*, and renders "votive offerings."

Regarding the meaning of the verb preceding *taklîme*, and upon which so much depends, I confess to being in puzzling doubt. The most natural reading is *ṣu-uḫ-mut*—the Shafel of *ḫamâtu*, glow or burn,[1] but *šu-uḫ-mud* is also possible, and from II R 22, 63, it is seen that the Assyrian really had a verb *ḫamâdu*. (Strass AV, 3154). Unfortunately, the vocabulary in which it occurs is badly mutilated, and it is quite impossible to conjecture from the group of words there mentioned what the force of *ḫamâdu* is. If l. 64, *ṭa-a* [*bu*] were absolutely certain, something more definitely might be said than that some of the following words signify "strong," "pressed," and the like. As it is, we have only *ḫamuttu* as our guide, which Sayce (PSBA, XI, p. 336) derives from *ḫamâdu*, and renders quite satisfactorily—judging from the context—as "gift." It is with considerable reserve, and only after long deliberation, that I venture to suggest the meaning "presentation" for the verb in our passage, which in connection with "offerings" and "give" of the following line seems to me to accord with the context.

13. For the expression *ina la adannišu*, of so frequent occurrence in astronomical texts, see Delitzsch., *Woert.*, p. 135, though it is questionable whether he is right in deriving *adannu*[2] from

[1] In the hymn ZA. IV, p. 11, 14 and the fourth creation tablet, l. 40, are examples of the Shafel of this verb.

[2] See my remarks, Proc. Am. Phil. Ass, 1887, p. xiii. Haupt (*Beitraege z. Assyr.* I, p. 120) derives the word from a stem *mediae waw* and compares Hebrew noun-forms like *lâšôn*

the stem, *êdû*. The phrase appears to have been used originally for unseasonable events happening *previous* to the expected time, and it is probably owing to this *nuance* that it interchanges with *ina la minâtišu* "against calculations," while in the course of further development along this line it acquired the force "in former times," (so *e.g.*, VR 65, col. I, 22), and then quite indiscriminately "out of season," with *ina la simânišu* as a synonym. See now also Jensen, *Kosmologie*, etc., p. 415. The trace of a sign which might be *nu* is to be seen at the end of this line.

14. *Cf.* "Black Stone," of Esarhaddon, IR 49, col. I, 21, where Marduk, enraged at the events in Babylonia, is spoken of *ana sapan mati ḫulluḳu nišê iktapud*, "planning the destruction of the land and the annihilation of men."

15–16. The unmistakable signs for "*šarru*" here[1] determine definitely the reading IR 66, obv. 24 f., 29 e., Rev. 27 b., and IR 34, 135, as *Ea šarru*, and not *man* as Thiele, *Gesch.*, p. 519, and others believe. With our passage as a variant, Thiele's conjectures and theories as to the identity of *Ea-mannu* and *Šulmanu*, based upon I R 23, 135, also fall to the ground. Peiser (K. B. I., p. 96), while also reading *mannu*, yet suggests in a note that *nu* may be a clerical error for *aḫu*, in which case, he says, we would be obliged to read *šarru*. Why may we not read simply *šarrunu* "our King"? If a clerical error exists, I should certainly seek for it in the repetition of *nu* after *Gu-la*. At all events, there can no longer be any question as to the reading of *šarru* in all these passages.

Ea evidently calls upon his son and servant, Marduk, to oppose the evil for the removal of which he has been appealed to. In view of the double sense of *amatu*, as "order" and "report," there may be some hesitation between rendering "Ea . . . . spread the report," or "Ea gave the command," but the latter is the more probable. The only other point here calling for remark is the ideograph EN-NA=*adi*. It is certainly rather curious to meet with this in a text distinguished for its preponderating "phonetic" style, and while EN occurs very often in Assyrian texts,

[1] The same in the Hymn published ZA., IV, p. 8 (l. 22).

the addition of the phonetic complement[1] suggests a different explanation, upon which I shall touch at the conclusion of my article.

17. For the verb *banû* in combination with *ṣalmu* instead of the more common and usual *êpêšu* or *nazâzu*, see Asurn. II, 133 *ṣalam Ninib . . . abnî*, and Tigl. Pil. III, II R 67, 81 *ṣalam abnî*. The form *abnû* with overlapping vowel is due to the relative clause (Delitzch *Gram.*, p. 147). The ordinary plural form of *ṣalmu* is *ṣalmânu*, but of course a second plural, *ṣalmê*, is legitimate.[2] Still, it is not altogether certain whether the plural is here intended, for *ṣa-al-me* may be used as the singular nominative, as the gloss., II R. 49, No. 3, 42, shows, and so it is likely also that II R 45, 54e *ṣalme* is a nominative as the preceding words are. To add to the confusion, *ṣalmu* seems to be indifferently used for singular or plural. Certainly II R 67, 81, the plural is intended, as the suffix in *bûnšin* proves, and so, too, there can be no doubt that *ṣalam ilâni rabûtê* (Layard, *Inscriptions*, etc., pl. 19, 4), refers to several images. The context leads me to believe that several images are spoken of in our text also.

18. For *la i-ir-ru*, and the meaning here assigned to it, compare the similar phrase, IV R 1, 34–36b. *Ištar ša ana ḳibîtiša Annunâki ištanu la i-ir-ru*—"*Ištar*, against whose command not a single one of the Annunaki stirs." For the stem see Delitzch *Woert.*, p. 358. At the end of the line some verb with the meaning "endowed" is no doubt to be supplied; also verbs of a similar meaning are demanded at the ends of the two following lines. The parallelism of itself suggests that *išdu* is a noun, and more especially a part of the body. While in his *Lesestuecke*, Schrifttafel No. 128, Delitzsch appears to restrict *išdu* to the sense of "foundation," and adopts the reading *šûnu* when the ideograph stands for "limbs" or "loins," in his *Grammar*, p. 26, No. 83, he includes the latter under the reading *išdu*. Our passage furnishes a further support for the double usage of *išdu*, and incidentally shows that we would be justified in reading the

[1] Strassmaier (quoted by Delitzsch *Woert.*, 372), reads EN-NA=*adi* in the sense of "and," but this is more than doubtful.

[2] Jensen, in *Keilschr. Bibl.* II, p. 206, (l. 48), adopts a plural *ṣalme*.

same way in the *Descent of Ištar*, Obv. 35, and Rev. 21. Whether Delitzsch adopts this reading already in his *Assyr. Studien*, p. 121–22, note[1], is not altogether clear, but certainly as much may be said in favor of this reading as for *šûnu*, which is adopted by Jeremias, *Vorstellungen*, etc., pp. 12 and 18, chiefly in view of II R 35, No. 4, ll. 63 and 67. To determine the meaning of this word, the passage VR, 25, 2 c-d must be taken into consideration, and from this passage I think it is clear that our word has become a legal term to express the *coitus*. In II R 35, it has a similar force, while ASKT., 118, Rev. 5, it stands in parallellism with *birku*, "knee." May it not be that *šûnu* are the *genitalia* proper, while *išdu* are the loins?

21. The expression *uznî išrukšunute* is evidently but a variant for the phrase *uznâ . . . išrukušu* occurring in the colophon attached to the tablets of *Ašurbanabal's* library. Compare also Haupt, *Nimrodepos*, p. 5, 41, *Ea urappišu uzunšu*, and also a lengthier phrase, II R 67,67, *ina uznî nikilti ḫasîsi palkî ša išruka abkallu ilu rubâ Ea*, etc.

22. *Šukuttu* has attained an extended use in Assyrian, as is but natural that a word with so general a meaning as "fabric" should. II R 67, 28, and elsewhere, it is applied to a product made of gold; I R 13, 66, of iron, and V R 6, 12, it is introduced to describe precious stones, and assuming the same reading *ib.* 16, which appears almost certain, the word is used in connection with the garment that betokens royalty. Jensen (*Keilschr. Bibl.* II, p. 204, note) questions the correctness of Amiaud's deductions (*Zeits. f. Keilschr.*, I, 251–2), that would establish for the word also the meaning of a dwelling, more particularly, "tabernacle," but there is certainly no reason, *à priori*, why *sukuttu* should not be applied to an edifice. I am strongly inclined to believe that VR 6, 45, Amiaud is right in his interpretation. At all events, the *šukuttê* there mentioned, together with the *namkûru* and the holy vessels, form part of the worship of the gods, and it is such a *šukuttu* which is certainly referred to in our

[1] He there reads *išit*, and proposes an etymology which no doubt he has long since abandoned.

passage. A confirmation of this view is furnished by the verb *ušanbiṭu*, which is invariably used in connection with constructions, (Nebuch., E.I.H., II, 45; T.P.III, II R 67, 82, and Nabonid, V R 64, II 13.)

23. Sayce, in his *Hibbert Lectures*, p. 310, reads the name of the plague-god *Nerra*, without, however, stating the grounds upon which he does so. Jensen (Z.A., I, p. 56) declares the "non-Semitic" pronunciation to have been Girra or Mirra, while in his recent work (*Kosmologie d. Babylonier*, p. 145 and 445), he wavers between Ura and Gira. From the fact that the sign No. 250 of the *Schrifttafel* has the phonetic value *ne* (S^2, 14), which is evidently curtailed from *nêru* (yoke) shown by S^2, 11, to be one of the meanings of the ideograph, it would seem but proper to conclude from II R 59, 46, that the name of the god was Ne-ra or Nerra, and not Gira, as Jensen believes; but the fatal objection against supposing this to be the Assyrian name of the god is that the column in which it occurs is clearly "non-Semitic." Jensen seems to appreciate the weakness of his position in ZA, I, p. 57, but in his *Kosmologie* makes no reference to the difficulty. After all, we are not much nearer a solution at present than we were at the time when George Smith published his *Chaldæan Genesis*, where, starting from the passage II R 25, $13,^{g-h}$ he read the name of the deity *Lubara*, and for which Delitzsch. (Germ. Edition, p. 309), suggested as a preferable reading *Dibbarra*, connecting it with the Hebrew *dĕbĕr*, pestilence. The objections against regarding the passage adduced by Smith as final are too obvious to be stated, but still it is the best evidence for the actual pronunciation that is as yet forthcoming. I do not see how Jensen can afford to ignore this passage altogether, and pending the final solution, which is not possible with the insufficient material at our disposal, I retain, provisionally, Delitzsch's reading of the name.

In view of IV R 5, col. I, 67, my conjecture at the end of this line stands assured. See, also, the Creation fragment, K, 3561, 14.

24. *Uzuz* might, of course, be the imperative Kal of

nazâzu, but since the context argues against this supposition, we must take it as the singular corresponding to the plural *uzuzzu*, which occurs IV R 5, col. I, 67.

From S. 954, Obv. 4 (Del. AL.[3], p. 134), where *Ištar* is addressed *ina irṣiti ina uzûziki*, there can be no further question as to the existence of an infinitive form, *uzûzu*,[1] to which *uzûz* and *uzuzzu* would be the third person singular and plural permansive, respectively. Furthermore, the ideographic equivalent in the two passages, IV R and S. 954, apart from other considerations, point unmistakably to a stem, *nazâzu*, but Delitzsch (*Gram.*, p. 276) can hardly be right in claiming the infinitive *uzûzu* to be a form derived from the Shafel *ušêziz*. It seems much more natural and simpler to regard *uzûzu* as a somewhat irregular form for the Infinitive Piel of the stem, which ought to be written *uzzuzu*. *Uzuz* and *uzzuzu* would then be permansives, following the analogy of this infinitive form.

25. If my reading at the end of the line be correct, *malikut* would either be a second plural for *maliku* by the side of *malike* (TP. I, 35), or the abstract noun, as *malikutu*, in the fourth tablet of the creation series, PSBA. X, 86, pl. I, 2.

IV.

Coming to the interpretation of the fragment, we find that it begins with an account of the destruction of a city by some agent. What is intended by the contrast between the animals of the mountain and of the field is not altogether clear. The former are represented as being caught by the destroyer—to speak thus indefinitely for the present—on his approach to the city, while it may be that those of the field are spared, though upon what grounds such a possible distinction is made is not apparent. It may be that there is some mythological allusion here which we will come across again in some other text, as yet unpublished. I find only one reference in a religious text which may possibly have some connection with the notion underlying

[1] Sayce, *Hibbert Lectures*, p. 464, very carelessly fails to distinguish between *izuz*, from a stem, *zizu*, and our *uzuzzu*, rendering both words by "*divide*."

our passage. In an incantation dealing with the disease *ṭi'u*[1] IV R 5, col. III, 15) there occurs the following phrase: *mamman la ibâšâ ištu šadî ušêrida.* Sayce's rendering (*Hibbert Lectures,* p. 461) is certainly wrong. The subject of *ušêrida* is, without much question, the disease, and *mamman la ibâšâ* I take as an idiomatic expression for "everything whatsoever"—the negative particle adding force just as it does in the idiomatic expression *mala bašu,*[2] "whatsoever." Graphically the various steps in the destruction of the city are described, and, upon the conclusion of his task, the destroyer proceeds to the "seat of the evil gods," which, as has been shown, is the expanse of heaven. The evil gods are the seven evil spirits to whom we have so many allusions in the religious texts, and since they are always represented as the enemies of mankind, we may conclude that it is not with hostile intent, but as belonging to their circle, that the destroyer now enters their midst. In other words, the mission upon which he has been sent out is completed, and he returns to present a report of his doings to the king of the evil spirits, Anu,—as one feels tempted to supply. The *ekallu* mentioned here would then refer to the palace of Anu in the heavens.

How many lines are missing at the end of the obverse must unfortunately remain an open question. A measurement of the clay library tablets, particularly those containing epic and religious texts, shows that the length of the tablets is pretty constant, and that the number of lines does not vary very much. Custom seems to have been as active a force in these matters in ancient Mesopotamia as it is to-day, in dictating the form of an 8vo or 12mo volume, and, indeed, with the manufacture of "writing" bricks carried on, on a large scale, which led no doubt to the use of molds, there is every reason to suppose that the sizes of the tablets were definitely fixed, and that the number of sizes in actual use was equally definite. Moreover, the systematic arrangement of a large library would of itself lead to the convenience of a "uniform binding" so far as this was possible, and it

1 According to Jensen, ZK., I, p. 303, "elephantiasis."
2 Compare the English idiom "never so great" by the side of "ever so great."

may be that under the additional influences of the natural conservatism of the East, *certain* shapes were always retained for certain *subjects*. Be this as it may, the average number of lines on a mythological or religious tablet may conveniently be put down as fifty to fifty-five. Now, since at the point where the obverse begins, the story appears pretty well advanced, ten to fifteen lines at least are to supplied at the beginning, which would leave about twenty lines to be added from the point where the obverse breaks off. But the difficulty in determining what connection exists between the obverse and reverse is enhanced by the impossibility of determining the original width of the tablet. That it consisted of several columns may be put down as almost certain, from the consideration that such is the case with almost all such tablets of *Ašurbanabal's* library as, like our own, contain a religious or mythological tale of some kind. The creation series of tablets, consisting, so far as at present ascertained, only of obverse and reverse, appear to form an exception, and so does the famous tablet recounting the story of the descent of *Ištar* into the world of spirits,[1] but the others, such as the *Gištubar* series, the "Dibbarra," the "Zu" series and so forth (*Cf.* Bezold *Babyl. Assy. Liter.*, pp. 175-176), consist of either four or six columns (that is, either two or three columns on each side), and so, also, the great magical texts have six columns. From the ease with which line 9 of reverse joins line 10, the breadth of each column can be approximately conjectured, but there are no means of ascertaining whether the tablet contained two or three columns on each side, though the chances are in favor of the former. What is left of the reverse in any case represents the last column of the brick. Now, with at least two columns entirely missing, it would of course be idle to speculate on the precise connection between the two sides, but assuming, as seems justifiable, some general connection, the reverse representing either the end of a story begun on the obverse, or the end of some episode belonging to a more extended epic, I find (*a*)

[1] It is to be noted that this tablet (IV R 31) is also distinguished by its quite exceptional length.

in the introduction of Ea and Marduk on the reverse, and (*b*) in the mention of the plague-god, the clue to the general interpretation of the fragment. In order to establish my position, it will be necessary to dwell at some length upon the character of Ea and Marduk in Babylonian mythology, as well as to make an attempt to trace the development of the rôles of both as revealed by the cuneiform literature.

The reverse begins, as already pointed out, with a petition addressed to various gods. Of these Ea responds and calls upon Marduk to undertake some work.

Now, Ea is, throughout the Babylonian religious and mythological literature, pre-eminently the "god of humanity." He is the creator of mankind. The favorite titles bestowed on him are "ruler of Humanity," "directing the destinies of men;"[1] the "giver of Laws." Accordingly, he is the saviour of mankind, who answers the appeal for help when it reaches him in his home in the watery abyss. When pestilence stalks about in the land, when disease enters the body, when disturbances in the natural phenomena strike terror into men's souls, it is to Ea that the petition for relief is sent. With him there is always associated from a certain period on, his son and servant, Marduk, who conveys the message of mankind to Ea, "dwelling in the watery abyss," and from Ea, Marduk receives orders and instructions how the evil complained of is to be removed. Precisely as in our text, so Ea is frequently portrayed as being roused to anger upon hearing of the ravages of the evil spirits, who are made responsible for everything. In a set speech he

[1] So I think, without much question, *naḳbu*, in the phrase, *muštêšir naḳbêšu* (Sargon, Cyl. 70, etc.), and *bêl naḳbi* (Sennacherib Bavian, l. 28) is to be rendered, and not "canal" or "source," as Lyon, Peiser, Winckler, Thiele (*Gesch.*, p. 519), and others do. Pognon, *Bavian*, p. 65, questions the correctness of the usual rendering, without suggesting any other. In a note to Dr. Ward's article on "The Rising Sun on Babylonian Cylinders," (*Jour. of American Archæology*, Vol. III, p. 56), I have suggested the same translation for *šad naḳbi*, "mountain of Fate," in VR 50, col. 1, l. 4, where the phrase stands in parallelism with *šad šimâtu*, and I connect the stem with Hebrew *nḳb*, "curse," a meaning that may be naturally developed from dwelling on the unfavorable side involved in the general conception of "fate." Thirdly, l. 20 of Fragment 18, I would render *naḳab limnuti, etc.*, "through whose (*i. e.*, Marduk's), pure incantation, evil destinies, are removed." I reserve a fuller proof for another occasion. (See now Jensen, *Kosmologie*, p. 362).

usually prescribes certain remedies which Marduk thereupon brings to mankind, or himself applies. The introduction of Ea and Marduk of itself makes it very likely that our fragment deals with a contest of some destructive power or powers against *men*. Were it a contest among the gods, it is almost certain that Bel, or Bel and Nusku would be introduced at this point, who bear about the same relation to the gods that Ea and Marduk do to men. Bel is pre-eminently the counsellor of the gods, and Nusku is his servant, ready to do his word. Hence the opposition between Bel and Ea, which is well brought out in the Babylonian version of the flood. Curiously enough, in the Deluge story, neither Bel nor Ea are accompanied by their servants. In contradistinction to what we find elsewhere, Ea communicates the decision of the gods directly to his favorite *Ṣitnapištim*, and not through the mediation of Marduk, and so there is no mention of Nusku in the story. Bel is the first to see the ship which has survived the general destruction; but the message of the survival is not conveyed to him by Nusku. I believe that we have here a means of fixing the comparative age of some of the mythological tales in the cuneiform literature, and, at the same time, an indication of their growth. Adopting the principle now generally admitted in the study of comparative mythology, that the simpler version is the older, the Deluge story in its original shape, at least, would belong to an earlier mythological stratum than such a fragment as ours, where the rescue of humanity is complicated by the mediation of Marduk. How the latter came to be added, and similarly why Nusku was attached to Bel, is a question into which it is impossible and needless to enter here. Suffice it to express in a word my conviction that the combination is due in both cases to an amalgamation of two deities, whose worship originated at different places, but whose character was very much alike. In the case of Ea and Marduk, the further suggestion may be permitted that the former, whose home is the ocean, was the "god of humanity" to a people living at the sea coast; the latter to a people whose seat was inland. A third period in the development of Ea-Marduk and Bel-Nusku myths is represented by portions of the text IV R 5, where, by the same process which led to attaching Marduk to Ea and Nusku to Bel, a combination of all four has taken place. Bel and Ea are no longer in opposition, but the former (IV R 5, col. I, 54 ffg), consults *with* Ea upon hearing of the ravages of the evil spirits. The words in which the anger of Bel is described are almost identical (see the commentary above) with those applied to Ea on other occasions. More remarkable still in the same text, col. ii, 32, ffg where the tale of the seven spirits is repeated, the news of their mischief first reaches Bel, who orders his servant Nusku to inform Ea "in the deep," whereupon the latter summons his son and servant, Marduk, and communicates in turn the news to him, at the same time taking the necessary steps for quelling the rebellion which the evil spirits have stirred up.

While, as a matter of course, I do not regard the different layers of these myths which I have pointed out as exhaustive or final—and, indeed, any "final" conclusion is impossible in the present state of our knowledge of Babylonian mythology, with hundreds of texts still obscure and so many more unpublished—I believe that the distinctions laid down merit attention, and, at all events, represent the method by means of which we may hope to obtain a picture of the unfolding and growth of this mythology.

Returning now to our text, and adopting provisionally the three distinguishable stages of the Ea myth, viz.:

(1) Ea, by himself, as saviour of humanity, opposed to Bel, as protector of the gods.

(2) Combination of Ea and Marduk, corresponding to the combination of Bel with Nusku.

(3) Amalgamation of Ea-Marduk with Bel-Nusku,

it is evident that the fragment before us belongs to the second stage.

Ea calls in the aid of Marduk, but it is to be noted that Ea *hears* the appeal directly, in contradistinction to the incantation texts, where Marduk *brings* him the news; and, secondly, a new feature in our fragment is the introduction of the armies of

Marduk. I am not aware of any other reference to these armies in the mythological literature. Elsewhere, in the fourth creation tablet, recounting the contest between Marduk and the dragon Tiamat, the weapons of Marduk are introduced, but neither here nor in the poetic fragment II R 19, No. 2, which is devoted to a detailed description of the equipment of the god, is there any mention made of his armies.[1] For this reason alone, any attempt to bring our Marduk into some connection with the vanquisher of Tiamat, which would naturally be suggested by the similarity of their rôles, must be abandoned; but there are also other considerations which show very clearly that the Marduk-Tiamat epic belongs to an entirely different series of myths.

Here it is at the command of Anu that Marduk undertakes the contest, and it is from Anu that he receives his weapons. In the body of the story Ea is not introduced at all, and indeed it would seem that not only has the Marduk of the "Dragon" epic nothing in common with the Marduk of our fragment and the other tales above referred to, but the introduction of Marduk into the "Dragon" story seems to be due to a later phase which the tale assumed, whereas the original and real hero is the god Bel, whose name, it is to be noted, constantly interchanges in the tale with Marduk. That the story in the form in which it is found in the so-called fourth tablet of the creation series (published by Budge, PSBA, x, p. 86) has been considerably modified from its original form by some redactor, or by the natural development of popular traditions, is clear from the attempt made in the closing lines to drag Ea into the story. The episode terminates properly with l 7, Rev. of Budge's text (Sayce's translation, *Hibbert Lectures*, p. 383, l. 1). What follows is merely a brief recapitulation and summary of the story, with the evident purpose, as shown by the concluding words, to bring it into relationship with the creation of the firmament, but with which I feel convinced it had *originally* nothing to do. This summary is introduced by the statement that since

[1] Tiamat appears to have forces at her command, in addition to *Kingu*, her husband, if the words *miḫru* and *puḫru* (Del., AL[3], p. 99, l. 23) are correctly interpreted by Sayce (*Hibbert Lectures*, p. 382).

the time that Marduk overcame Tiamat, the lamentations of Ea ceased, and again, further on, it is said that Marduk, after the contest, presented himself before the deep, the seat of Ea.[1] But it is Anu who orders the combat, and accordingly we should expect the hero to present his account to this god. Evidently this addition and change has been made at a time when Marduk was inseparably joined to Ea as his special messenger, while in the story itself Marduk has taken the place which originally belonged to Bel, who, as already said, is pre-eminently the warrior of and for the gods. Again, we may further distinguish between redactions of the story in which Bel still occurs by the side of and interchangeably with Marduk, and those in which the latter has completely usurped the rôle of the former, and where, moreover, Anu also disappears to make room for Ea. This is the case in the fragment No. 18, published by Delitzsch, AL.,[3] p. 95–96, which certainly treats of this conflict, the position of which fragment, therefore, in the creation series is not at all as clear as Jensen would have it. We may, accordingly, suppose the development of the story to have been somewhat as follows:

Originally, the Tiamat story represented a contest among heavenly spirits. Bel, as the warrior of the gods, is commanded by Anu, the king of the gods, to wage war against the dragon. He succeeds, and upon the completion of the struggle presents himself before Anu. Through the amalgamation, probably, of the worship of Bel with Marduk, for which we have satisfactory evidence,[2] Marduk is introduced into the story as identical with Bel, whose name, under the form of *be-lu* (signifying "lord") becomes a mere title of Marduk. The association of Marduk with Ea leads to the introduction of the latter, and in consequence the character of Tiamat is transformed. From being the enemy of gods, she becomes the enemy of men, and this leads naturally to the substitution of Ea for Anu as the instigator of the combat, and the complete usurpation on the part of Marduk of the rôle belonging to Bel. While, therefore, as stated

[1] Written in both cases ideographically NU GIM-MUD.

[2] Fully set forth by Sayce, *Hibbert Lectures*, pp. 92–108, though his view of the original character of Marduk is untenable.

at the outset of this discussion, the vanquisher of Tiamat must be kept distinct from the Marduk of our fragment, still the reference to his armies and the allusion to a combat suggests that the rôle in which Marduk is represented arose under the same influence that produced the form he has assumed in the Tiamat epic, in what I regard as its transformed phase. Again, in the "incantation" texts, it is by procuring waters of purification, or by prescribing magic formulæ, that Marduk succeeds in redeeming man from the ravages of the evil spirits, and even in the case of the revolt of the heavenly bodies it seems that the mere word of Ea, is sufficient to re-establish peace and order. There is no allusion to a combat, nor any reference to armies. Ea is a god like the one pictured by the prophet Zechariah, 4, 6, who acts "not by force nor by might," but by his "word"[1] sent out through Marduk, and I should like to suggest that the character of the latter, more specifically as a warrior with armies at his back, is due to his absorption of the rôle of Bel, and does not appear, therefore, until the amalgamation and identification of Bel[2] with Marduk has taken place.

Returning now to our fragment, we will be in a position, despite the obscurity enveloping the lines that follow upon the announcement of Ea's wrath, to determine the general trend of the narrative. In the commentary, we have called attention to parallel passages where the anger of Ea is described. Taking these up again, and bearing in mind the conclusions we have reached regarding the development of what we may for convenience call the "Ea myth," it is clear that the reverse of the fragment introduces some variation of the well-known Ea-Marduk episode that we meet with so frequently. As in the several passages above discussed, and elsewhere, so here Ea has been appealed to, and in response, calls upon his son, Marduk, to undertake some task. To briefly recapitulate, we find this episode

[1] One cannot help thinking of the *d'bar Jahwê*, "word of Jahwê," which plays an equally important part in a certain stage of the religion of the Hebrews.

[2] It is worthy of note, as pointing to their antiquity, that in the Babylono-Assyrian Hemerologies, Anu and Bel are associated together, never Anu and Marduk. *Cf.* Sayce, *Hibbert Lectures*, pp. 70-76.

between Marduk andEa twice referred to at some detail in the magical text IV R 5, Cols. I and II. In both instances it is against the ravages of the seven evil spirits that the help of Ea is solicited, and, in fact, the second account, Col. II, is but a repetition, with some variations, of the account in Col. I. A general disturbance of the heavenly bodies has taken place. The Moon-god has been eclipsed. *Šamas* and *Ramman* have deviated from their paths, and *Ištar*, with *Anu*, is in rebellion. Ea, upon hearing the news, is enraged, and calls upon Marduk to fight the evil spirits, upon the termination of which *Sin*, *Šamas*, *Ramman*, *Ištar* and *Anu* are fixed in their places as before "night and day without interruption." Again, in the magical text IV R 15, Ea, upon the request of the fire-god, abetted by Marduk, stops the ravages of these spirits. In both texts the story is introduced in the midst of incantations, or followed by incantations. Thirdly, in a large number of instances (IV R 3, cols. I, 31 II, 2; 4, col. III, 23; 50 col. II, 41, etc., etc.), an abbreviated form of a similar episode is found where, upon the request of Marduk, who informs his father of some evil that has afflicted a person, the god of humanity gives his son the necessary instructions for the cure of the trouble. It is needless for our purposes to dwell on the fact that Ea is represented here as interfering both on behalf of gods and men. If the deductions above made are correct, the explanation for this double rôle is to be sought in the absorption on the part of Ea of the rôle which belonged originally to Bel; but what is essential, is the circumstance that in all the passages in which the episode in any form has hitherto been found, it has been introduced incidentally—a quotation, as it were— for the purpose evidently of justifying the appeal to Ea by means of incantations; just as the episode of the descent of *Ištar* to the lower world is recited with a view of justifying the belief in the possibility of a return of the spirits from their dark and dreary dungeon.[1] In the text before us, however, the episode evidently forms *part* of the narrative which the tablet contained, and it is this direct allusion that lends to it a special interest and importance, as will appear presently.

[1] See Jeremias' *Babyl-Assyrisch Vorstellungen*, etc., pp. 6-8.

The questions now arise, against whom is Ea's wrath directed, and for what purpose are the armies of Marduk called into requisition? The answer to these questions I find in the reference to the plague-god, toward the end of the reverse. Attention has already been called to the expression used, IV R 5, col. I, 67, in connection with the revolt of the heavenly bodies of *Sin*, *Šămas* and *Ištar*. We there read: *muša u urra uzuzzu la naparkăšunute*, that "day and night they were fixed without interruption." So it was before the revolt took place, and so, again, after the rebellion has been quelled. In our text it is Dibbarra who is described as being "fixed day and night without interruption." It is certainly but legitimate to conclude, from this, that it is against Dibbarra that the efforts of Ea and Marduk are directed, as a result of which he is firmly chained to his place, and restrained from doing the mischief upon which, according to Babylonian mythology, he is always bent. Precisely, then, as in the Marduk-Ea episodes with the seven evil spirits, with the heavenly bodies and with the various evils (superinduced by the spirits) afflicting mankind, it is through the agency of the god of humanity, in consort with his son, that the violence of the plague-god is checked. I conclude, therefore, that we have on the reverse of our fragment a scene in a narrative which described some of the ravages of the plague-god, ending with the final subjugation of the latter through Ea and Marduk. Assuming, furthermore, as we found justifiable, some connection between the obverse and reverse, it is Dibbarra who is the subject of the verbs with which the obverse begins. He it is who enters the city of Inmarmaru and brings about its destruction. But, again, just as in the story of the heavenly revolt, the seven evil spirits are the instigators of the movement, so behind Dibbarra there is another and greater power, at whose command, it would appear, the destruction is undertaken—Anu, the king of the gods, the same as whose "messengers" the seven spirits commit their deeds of violence and destruction. It is to Anu, therefore, as I take it, that Dibbarra, after finishing the mission (or a part of it) on which he has been sent, proceeds with a report of his doings. After this it is likely that further ravages of Ḍibbarra were recounted; but leaving this and all other conjectures aside for the present, it is against the plague-god that the appeal to the deities mentioned on the reverse is made. Who the person or persons are presenting the petition, whether the inhabitants of Iṇmarmaru or some other place, it is, of course, idle to conjecture. That neither *Sin*, *Šamas* nor *Ištar* responds is quite in accord with the position occupied by these deities in IV R 5, ranged, as they there are, against Ea and Marduk, and acting in union with Anu and the evil spirits. Before proceeding here to a discussion of other tales—or, rather, fragments of tales—in which Dibbarra appears in a rôle similar to that of our fragment, and which will, I trust, more firmly establish the interpretation proposed, it is necessary to dwell on the references to the "offerings," and the "images" that follow upon the announcement of Ea's wrath. Beginning with the former, it is worthy of notice, as throwing, perhaps, some light on the difficulty, that in the two hymns quoted in the commentary to the word *taklîme* Marduk is addressed as the one who "gives gifts or offerings," and so in a third hymn, published by Brünnow ZA. V, pp. 77–78), K, 7592, Rev. 11, Marduk is said to be *nâdin kitruba u nindâbu*[1] *ana il*—"giving sacrifice and free-will offering to the god . . . . ;" and where the parallelism *mukîn têrit apsî*, "establishing the law of the watery deep" (the home of Ea), suggests the restoration "Ea." Is there, perhaps, some allusion to these "gifts" in our tablet, or have we a more general reference to offerings that were made at an improper season? From the Babylo-Assyrian hemerologies we see that as there were certain days on which sacrifices were brought, there were others on which they were expressly forbidden. Thus, in a hemerology for the month of Elul (translated by Sayce, *Hibbert Lectures*, pp. 70–76) there is an injunction against offerings on the 7th, 14th, 19th, 21st and 28th day of the month. At all events, so much is clear that there is a reference here to offerings that

[1] Synonyms, it will be remembered, of *taklîmu*, V R II, 1–2. See Sayce, *Hibbert Lectures*, p. 73, note.

were given at an improper time, and it furthermore appears legitimate to conclude that, in consequence of this transgression, a destruction of lands and men had been ordered. It is hardly to be supposed, however, that it is Ea or Marduk who instigates this terrible destruction, but either Anu, or Dibbarra at the command of Anu. These lines, then, furnish the explanation for the wrath of Ea, and it is not until the fifteenth line, where the latter utters the great "word" (as in IV R 3, col. II, 22), that Ea begins to act.[1] I venture to suggest further that it is the inhabitants of some city who have offended Anu by offering sacrifices at an improper season, and in consequence of which they, just as Inmarmaru, have been visited by the plague-god. They appealed to various deities, and Ea responds.

Passing on now to the reference to the "images," the following passages in mythological texts are to be taken into consideration:

There is an allusion to the images of Ea and Marduk in the "prescription" against evil spirits, IV R 21, No. 1, 38. As a means of protection, they are to be placed to the right and left of the gate, and further on (l. 41), Marduk is spoken of as *âšibu ṣalam*[2] "inhabiting the image." Again, in K 1284 (published by Lenormant *Et Accad.*, II, p. 239), immediately after the usual Ea-Marduk dialogue, the order is given by Ea to Marduk, *ṣalam andunânišu*[3] *binî*, *i. e.*, "the image of his full height build."

Furthermore, from Sargon Bull., l. 71 (Gold inscrip. 19 ffg. Annals 424 and 429), it appears that a belief was current which made Ea the author of the colossi, stationed at the approaches to the palace chambers, as well as of sculptured images in general.[4] See II R where Ea, under the form of

[1] See below, p. 36, where the same phrase as in our text, *ana sapan matati*, with the probability of a restoration, *ḫulluḳ nišê*, is used of Dibbarra. Elsewhere, Nergal, concerning whose identity with the plague-god, see below, p. 134–5, is spoken of as *sâpin mat nukurti* (IV R 26, No. 1, 29) and *sāpin mat la magiri* (IV R 24, 57).

[2] Compare the description of Jahwê *yošêb haḳ-ḳerûbîm* (1Kgs 8, 7, etc., etc.), K 7592, Rev. 7, Marduk is spoken of *âšib parakki*.

[3] I think we may finally settle upon *andunânu* as being a synonym of *bunânu*. See Zimmern, *Busspś*. Note 1.

[4] See Thiele Gesch., p. 520.

Nin-a-gal, is defined as *ilu ša nappâḫi*, "god of the smithy"—a sort of Babylonian Vulcan.

Now it seems to me that there must be some allusion in our text to these images, which even in later times, when the belief in their divine origin was no longer current, were supposed to grant protection against evil spirits.[1] Further than this general proposition, however, that Ea who, I take it, is here speaking, refers to some image or images that he has made, it is hardly possible to go. The suffix *šunu*, would lead us to suppose that they have been already referred to. May it be that there was an account of their having been destroyed by Dibbarra, in the course of his ruthless passage from city to city, and that Ea now gives the order to Marduk and his armies to restore them? Such a train of reasoning would further lead us to see in the *šukuttu* something connected with these images—a "tabernacle," as Amiaud has it, the destruction of which must also have been recounted in the last portion of the tablet, and which is now likewise being rebuilt. Thirdly, the "house" (l. 25), which is added to the *šukuttu*, would be the temple proper encompassing the *ṣalme* and *šukuttu*, and we would thus have in the images, tabernacle and temple a description passing from the smaller to the greater. Who the speakers in l. 26 are, whether Ea and Marduk, or Marduk and his hosts, or what not, it is impossible to say, but there will hardly be any question that the warning, "do not thou approach," is directed against Dibbarra. There would thus be a direct allusion to an attack made at some time upon the temple, and by the plague-god. Through the express indication that the images were built "amongst men," equivalent in force here to "for the benefit of men," the supposition that the scenes of destruction recounted on the tablet take place on earth, and not among the heavenly bodies, receives a further support. Finally, in connection with the binding of Dibbarra to his proper place "night and day without interruption," attention might be called to another passage in the hymn to Marduk, K 7592, Rev. 4, *šumêlaka Dibbarra rabû*

[1] *E. g.*, Tigl Pil III, II R 67. 81, builds images *maṣar šut ilâni rabûte*, as "a protection on the part of the great gods." Why Schrader (*Keils Bibl.*, II, p. 24), reads *zar-šu-ut*, which he is unable to translate, I do not know. See now Thiele ZA. V, p. 302.

dandan ilâni panûkka: "At thy left (O Marduk) (stands) Dibbarra, the great, the strongest of the gods, before thee." The passage besides containing a reference to a subjugation of the plague-god by Marduk, suggests the restoration proposed at the end of l. 25.

V.

To pass on now to the relationship existing between our fragment and other portions of the mythological literature of the Babylonians, we have in Smith's *Chald. Genesis,*[1] pp. 110–119, the remains of an epic devoted to the deeds of Dibbarra. Unfortunately, the texts themselves there translated by Smith-Delitzsch, have never been published, and that renderings made almost fifteen years ago are no longer reliable, need hardly be said. Sayce appears to have consulted some of these texts for his *Hibbert Lectures* (pp. 310-13) and offers revised translations of some lines. He has not, however, attempted any classification of the fragments beyond the one made by George Smith, which was as satisfactory as was possible under the circumstances.

There is every reason to hope that among the thousands of fragments from *Ašurbanabal's* library still unpublished and unexamined in the British Museum, further portions of the epic will be forthcoming, and we may confidently look forward for some valuable light on the subject from Dr. Bezold's *Catalogue of the Koujunijik Collection,* now in course of preparation;[2] but pending a gathering of all the fragments and a new study of those translated by Smith from the original tablets, which I hope to undertake at no distant day, it would only be idle and profitless conjecture to attempt any reconstruction of the divisions of the epic. We are, however, in a position at the close of our study of the interesting fragment, however unsatisfactory it is in many respects, to assert the close connection of our fragment

[1] I quote the German Edition of Friedr Delitzsch, Leipzig, 1876.

[2] In Vol. I of the Catalogue (1889), p. 258, there is a description of K 1282 belonging to the series. Another fragment is M. 55, Sayce, *Hibbert Lectures*, p. 311; Delitzsch. *Woert.*, p. 558.

with those found in Smith-Delitzsch and Sayce. A brief reference to the contents will show this very clearly. Smith gives four fragments. In the fragment which Smith takes as the beginning of the epic, the order is given to Dibbarra by Anu to destroy the entire human race.[1] In a second fragment, the translation of which is the most unsatisfactory of all, Ea is introduced. The third, which consists of four columns (M 55), describes in great detail Dibbarra's ravages in Babylon, Erech, Duran (?), Kutha, and a large number of the towns on all sides of Babylonia, which in succession seem to be the object of the divine wrath. Here, as well as in the fourth fragment (K 1282), which has attached to it a colophon, stating that it is the fifth tablet of a series, Dibbarra is accompanied by his servant *Išum*. There is a reference in the third fragment to the wrath of Marduk, though no mention of Ea occurs in what is published. In the fifth tablet, reverse, Dibbarra is spoken of as having the intention "*ana sapan matati*," Marduk [son of Ea], is sent out "at the beginning of the night," and the tablet ends with the hope that Dibbarra may be eternally appeased.

The points of comparison which justify the designation of our fragment as a portion of the Dibbarra epic are then briefly as follows:

1. Anu as the probable instigator of the destruction.
2. Dibbarra as the agent.
3. The wrath directed against the city.
4. The reference to the destruction of lands and annihilation of men.
5. The introduction of Ea and Marduk.
6. The mission of Marduk.
7. The appeasing of Dibbarra's violence.

It is needless for our purposes to dwell on the original character and development of Dibbarra and of his relation to Nergal, particularly as a portion of the subject has recently been fully and very satisfactorily treated by Jensen, *Kosmol-*

[1] The term used is *ṣalmat ḳaḳḳadi*, "black-headed," an expression synonymous with "humanity." Compare the corresponding phrase in our text, "destruction of lands and annihilation of men."

ogie d. Babylonier, pp. 476–90. I accept his theory of the identification of Dibbarra and Nergal at a very early period in Babylonian mythology, though of course the two deities must originally have been distinct. In this connection there is only one point to which, on account of its general bearings on the Dibbarra epic, I desire to call attention here. Above I have given my reasons for preferring the reading *Ner* or *Nerra* as the "non-Semitic" designation of the plague-god. The god Nergal is evidently nothing but the "great Ner." Now, on the supposition that Dibbarra represents the "small Ner," we would have an explanation for the fact that he is represented by an ideograph which has the meaning "servant." In other words, Nergal and Nerra bear the same relation to one another that afterwards applies to *Nerra and Išum*,[1] viz., master and servant; and I take it that *Išum* was introduced by the side of Dibbarra after the latter's—or, as we might also put it, in consequence of the latter's—amalgamation with Nergal. Now, in some of the fragments of the Dibbarra epic published by Smith, *Išum* actually does appear as performing the will of Dibbarra, and it becomes at once evident that the epic assumed its definite state after Nergal and the plague-god proper had become completely identified. In the first and second of Smith's fragments, however, there is no reference to *Išum*; of course they are exceedingly fragmentary, but if it should turn out that Dibbarra acts by himself there as in our text, we would have two recensions of the "epic" with the introduction of *Išum* as an indication for the growth of the story, precisely as we have seen the association of Marduk with Ea marking a stage in the development of the "Ea myth." This association of two deities in Babylonian mythology bearing the relation of father and son, and corresponding to master and servant, such as Bel and Nusku, Ea and Marduk, Ner and Nergal, *Dibbarra and Išum*, is exceedingly curious and important, and deserves a more careful investigation than has as yet been accorded to it.

If a final suggestion of a general character be permitted, I

[1] *Išum* is invariably designated as the 'messenger' and 'lieutenant' of Dibbarra.

should say that the whole epic must have been divided into several distinct parts like the "*Gišṭubar*" story, each part containing some episode in the career of the plague-god, and all together constituting the series which formed a collection under the designation—to judge from the colophon to K 1282—"The Great Deeds of Dibbarra." The question as to the position of our fragment in the series must, of course, with the inadequate material at our disposal, be left for future consideration. Summing up, then, the conclusions reached, I claim that our fragment represents a portion of the "Dibbarra" epic, in which there is set forth the destruction of a city, Inmarmaru, by the god of pestilence, followed by further accounts of the ravages of the god—very likely the destruction of other cities, with their temples and images—until, upon a final appeal to the gods, Ea, in consort with Marduk, brings Dibbarra under subjugation and orders Marduk, with his hosts, to repair the damage that has been done; and, furthermore, our fragment stands in close connection with a series of other fragments that deal with the deeds of Dibbarra.

In conclusion, I wish to direct attention to an expression in our fragment, from which I venture to draw an important inference as to the original form of the narrative. In line 23, we find the order *muša u urra* "night and day." The observation has been made that in so-called Sumero-Akkadian texts, "night" precedes "day," whereas in the Assyrian "translation" it is just the reverse (see *e. g.*, KAT, p. 57 note, and quite recently Jensen, ZA V, p. 124). An examination of purely Assyrian texts bears out the view that the Assyrian order is "day and night," with a few exceptions. So in the historical texts, I find only two passages where we meet with the "Sumero-Akkadian" order, the one in the Nabonid cylinder (PSBA, January, 1889) col. I, 12, and the other in Sargon's Annals, l. 303, (ed. Winckler, p, 67), where, by a careless slip, Winckler, in his translation, turns the phrase around.[1] Otherwise we invariably find *immu u mušu*, or *urru u mušu* (*Cf.* Sarg. Cyl. 43 and 49;

[1] For explanation of these exceptions, see note to p. 40.

Prunkinschrift 190, Bull. 48, K 2867 (*Ašurbanabal*) Rev. 9, publ. by George Evans, *Essay on Assyriology*, appendix).[1] Again, in the Nimrod Epic, although of Babylonian origin, and, as I believe, very old, but whose late Assyrian redaction, under the influence of Assyrian ideas, is generally acknowledged, "day and night" is the invariable order (ed. Haupt, pp. 4, 45; 6, 38; 7, 7; 11, 21; 13, 19; 69, 20 and 23. Deluge, col. III, 19). On the other hand, in the interlinear renderings of "non-Semitic" texts, night invariably takes precedence, and this applies as well to texts whose "non-Semitic" side or column still exists, such as IV R. 5, cols. I, 67 and II, 23; 15, col. II, 19; 18 No. 1, 21; 19 No. 3, 59; 22, 8a; 27 No. 3, 31, as well as such in which the Assyrian "translation" alone is preserved, as in the Penitential Psalm, IV R, 26, No. 8, 59.[2] Would it not seem, therefore, that our text is to be placed in the same category as the psalm just referred to, namely, a text which presupposes the existence of a "Sumero-Akkadian" original, and that by a fortunate accident the original "Sumero-Akkadian" order of the phrase has been retained?

I have already referred (see comment to line 16 of reverse) to the ideograph EN-NA, occurring in our text, and have little hesitation now in seeing herein also an "untranslated" survival of the Sumero-Akkadian original. Thirdly, the form for *ra* in the spelling of the name *Dibbara*, as well as in *ušaḫrabu* (line 5

[1] See in general Delitzsch *Woert.*, p. 236.

[2] In the Assyrian astronomical reports, day is mentioned before night, as we would naturally expect, (*e. g.*, III R 51, Nos. 1 and 2) and this, in connection with the facts pointed out, suggests the conclusion that, whereas in Babylonia—the home of the religious literature—the official day began with sunset, in Assyria the point of departure for all calculations was sunrise, which carries with it the assumption that the popular custom was the same. Whether in later times, through the influence of Assyria, a change was introduced into Babylonia, is a question which I am not prepared to answer. In the two exceptions to the Assyrian order above noted, it is significant that the one occurs in the cylinder of a Babylonian king, and the other in the account of a Babylonian campaign, so that, unless it be supposed that these two exceptions are accidental, the legitimate conclusion seems to be that the old custom was preserved in Babylonia till the end of the empire. It may very well be also that both methods of reckoning the day existed side by side, the one as a survival, the other as an innovation, just as among the Jews in the post-exilic period there were two methods of calculating the year, one beginning in the Spring, which was a survival of the "agricultural" stage, the other beginning in the Fall, which was due to adoption from the Babylonians. See Jensen's remarks, ZAV, p. 123-4 [Epping's new work, *Astronomisches aus Babylon*, which probably throws more light upon this point, is not accessible to me.]

of the obverse) is distinctly Babylonian, and, according to Delitzsch, AL[3] p. 22, note 1, peculiar—to quote his exact words —"to North Babylonian texts, and copies of the latter, *e. g.*, in the legend of the god of Pestilence,[1] and almost constant in the bilingual Akkadic-Babylonian texts."[2] This again not only points to an original in the Babylonian variation of cuneiform script from which the scribes of *Ašurbanapal* made our copy, and therefore takes us to Babylonia as the home of the story, but furnishes an additional reason for conjecturing an earlier "Sumero-Akkadian" prototype. Finally, the introduction of the Ea-Marduk episode, which has, up to the present at least, been found only in "bilingual" texts, may serve as a further substantiation of this conjecture, though I am not willing, for obvious reasons, to lay any great stress upon this support.

If this conclusion be accepted, it carries with it the general theory that the entire "Dibbarra" epic is a Babylonian tale originally composed in the non-Semitic "style," but of which we have at present only fragments of the Assyrian "translation;" and there is the further probability that some of these fragments represent a later and independent Assyrian redaction, based upon the "non-Semitic" original.

APPENDIX.

NOTE BY LEE K. FRANKEL, B.S., UNIVERSITY OF PA.

The brick was found to be covered with a white layer which could be scratched very easily with a knife-blade, and even with the finger nail.

On further examination with the microscope, minute vitreous crystals could be observed, having apparently a monoclinic habitus, and were judged from their previously determined hardness to be crystals of selenite (gypsum). The greater portion of the incrustation, however, was of the massive variety.

[1] Incidentally another proof for the companionship of our text with the "Dibbarra" series.

[2] Also in the "*Gišdubar*" and "Deluge" texts. Haupt, *Beitr. fur Assyr.*, I, p. 70.

The brick was first suspended in dilute hydrochloric acid, its action upon the incrustation being, however, very slow.

Upon immersing the brick in concentrated hydrochloric acid better results were obtained.

The gypsum was gradually but completely dissolved out, requiring, however, considerable time, since it had settled into every portion of the sunken characters, and hence exposed but a small portion of its surface at a time to the action of the acid.

Hot concentrated hydrochloric acid was also tried, but its action was found to be too energetic, since it dissolved out very readily the ferric oxide present in the brick, with a corresponding removal of the reddish color from it.

The above action also took place on using the cold acid, but in a lesser degree.

It was found that after the acid had exercised its solvent and loosening power, the application of a tooth-brush over the surface of the brick removed the soft gypsum, still undissolved, very materially, leaving the harder clay inviolate. This was especially serviceable for the more minute characters.

A theory that could be suggested for the presence of the incrustation of gypsum on the brick, is that it existed as such in the ferruginous clays as found in the Southern countries of Mesopotamia; that on baking these clays it became converted into the anhydrous variety (anhydrite), which from continued exposure to air and moisture, dissolved and recrystallized as gypsum.

This is especially probable, since the gypsum appeared not only as an incrustation on the surface of the brick, but was found deposited throughout the whole body of it, and to such an extent that on immersing the greater portion of the brick in the acid, the dissolving gypsum had a tendency to effect the complete disintegration of the brick. It is advisable, therefore, so to suspend the brick in the strong acid that merely its surface comes in contact with the acid. If this precaution is followed, it is not likely that this treatment can effect any permanent or serious injury, but rather the reverse.

Publications of the University of Pennsylvania.

SERIES IN

Philology Literature and Archæology.

VOL. I.

1. Poetic and Verse Criticism of the Reign of Elizabeth. By FELIX E. SCHELLING, A.M., Assistant Professor of English Literature.......$1.00

2. A Fragment of the Babylonian "Dibbarra" Epic. By MORRIS JASTROW, Jr., Ph.D., Professor of Arabic.................................. .60

3. *a.* Πρός with the Accusative. *b.* Note on a Passage in the Antigone. By WILLIAM A. LAMBERTON, A.M., Professor of the Greek Language and Literature.. .50

4. The Gambling Games of the Chinese in America. Fán tán and Pák kòp piú. By STEWART CULIN, Secretary of the Museum of American Archæology.. .40

[In preparation.]

The Terrace at Persepolis. By MORTON W. EASTON, Ph.D., Professor of Comparative Philology.

An Aztec Manuscript. By DANIEL G. BRINTON, M.D., Professor of American Archæology and Linguistics.

A Monograph on the Tempest. By HORACE HOWARD FURNESS, Ph.D., LL.D.

Recent Archæological Explorations in New Jersey. By CHARLES C. ABBOTT, M.D., Curator of the American Collections.

Archæological Notes in Northern Morocco. By TALCOTT WILLIAMS, A.M., Secretary of the Museum of Egyptian Antiquities.

a. On the Aristotelian Dative. *b.* On a Passage in Aristotle's Rhetoric. By WILLIAM A. LAMBERTON, A.M., Professor of the Greek Language and Literature.

A Hebrew Bowl Inscription. By MORRIS JASTROW, Jr., Ph.D., Professor of Arabic.

The Life and Writings of George Gascoigne. By FELIX E. SCHELLING A.M., Assistant Professor of English Literature.

www.ingramcontent.com/pod-product-compliance
Lightning Source LLC
Chambersburg PA
CBHW021428090426
42739CB00009B/1404
9783337247126